A Girl With A Cape™

The true story about the superhero in all of us

Written by
Amy Logan

Published by
Full Heart Publishing

This book is dedicated to my family and friends for their incredible
support and encouragement, and all those who have helped me along the way.
Vince, Sadie & Scott, I love you very much.

And to all those who have ever felt, even for a second, that
they couldn't make a difference, this book is for you.
Please don't ever forget – the world needs you.

xo,

amy

Original illustrations by
Tracy Wendt
Illustrations digitally remastered by
Vince Logan
Copyright © 2013-2015
Title fonts courtesy of **Fontscafe.com**, Copyright 2012
Photo of Amy Logan courtesy of **Moments By A**, MomentsByA.com
Published by Full Heart Publishing, Full Heart, LLC
Printed in USA
Second edition, first print

ISBN-13: 978-0-9890465-2-7

GotYourCape.com

Can someone so small make a difference at all?
Can someone like you make the world seem brand new?
I'm not sure you know this, but I tell you it's true.
It's a story of a superhero... of a kid just like you.

So sit back, bundle up, take a breath...

......let it out...

A Girl With A Cape is what this is about.

Once upon a time, there was a girl with a cape...

Well not so much a cape, but a scarf that she tied,
but it *FELT* like a cape because she felt *SUPER* inside.

The girl knew something
that most never do.
She could change the world!
She knew that to be true,
but didn't know what, or how,
just *"There's more..."*

...which is why every day, the cape she wore.

Want to know what happened on Monday?

On Monday, she woke up refreshed and bright-eyed.
Ready to go, the scarf, she tied.
Brushed her teeth, ate her breakfast, her day ready to start...

then said, "*Mom I love you... with all of my heart.*"

Now what she **didn't** know
is mom felt pretty beat.
Sometimes moms feel that way
when they're always on their feet.
Mom was so tired and
wanted to go back to bed,

but the **I LOVE YOU** filled mom's heart,
so she did this instead...

She baked a cake,
went to the store,
bought stuff for dinner to cook some more.
She loved on the cashier
who was ready to quit,
and that sparked a smile that had never been lit.
The cashier was promoted
for helping with care.
Customers came far and wide to shop there
and all of the guests
left the store feeling great!

All from the "*I love you*" from the girl with the cape.

On Tuesday, the day started just like the last;
a kiss and a kind word to mom as she passed.

The girl went out searching for something SO GRAND;
to make the world *BETTER* is what she had planned.

Something **SO BIG** that would make her feel **tall**;
to make a BIG DIFFERENCE from a girl so small.

Because although she was little, she knew there was more, and in case **Tuesday** was the day, her tied scarf she wore.

Do you want to hear more of what she had in store?

On Wednesday,
she helped wash the dog head to tail.
She thanked the mail carrier for bringing the mail.
She made a nice note for the neighbor next door.
She held the door open for a kid at the store.

She said, "Please" and "Thank You" and "That's a nice hat,"
and all of a sudden, no sooner than that...

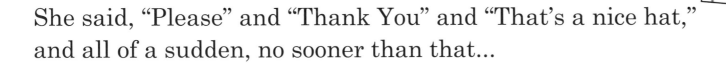

The kind words didn't stop — they continued to go on.
They traveled to the next guy,

the next one,

and so on...

"You are a great friend!"

"You are the best mom!"

"Would you like to join me for lunch?"

"Thanks for helping me."　　"I think you're great!"　　"You look so pretty today."

BUT...

She didn't see any of this magic take place.
To her, it was normal to put a smile on a face.

So...

On Thursday, she started to question the cape!

"HEY CAPE!!! What difference do YOU make?
I still have no powers! I'm no superhero!
What have I done? That's a big fat zero!
Nothing I tell you! Nothing at all!
I can't make a difference... I'm just way too small!"

Just then, mom came in to settle her down.
Her sadness was sad... a big old sad frown.

Mom said,
"I heard what you said,
and it's so not true.
The world is much better
and it's **because** of you...

Look!
The dog is now happy and smells even better.
The mailman whistles when bringing us letters.
The people at stores hold open the doors,

and that's just a couple of things, but there's more.

MY HEART *is so full from the things that you say.*
You tell me you love me, and ***THAT*** *makes my day.*
You ***ARE*** *a superhero, your* ***WORDS*** *are your cape.*
When you say kind things, it makes people feel great.

*And do you want to know something **MORE** that's outrageous?*

Your kind words and actions are truly contagious!

What you say matters and travels for miles.
Your one little sentence brings HUNDREDS of smiles.

Now **THAT'S** a super power — your words, what you say.

YOU have the power to brighten a day.
Yes, **YOU** are the biggest difference maker of all.

You may think you're small ,

but your words make you $TALL$.

Your **heart** and your **smile,**
you don't need a cape.
Your **actions** and **kindness,**
those things make you great!

So…

Now that you know that your powers are true…

tell me sweet darling,

...what next will you do?"